MW01712238

A Win-Win Solution:

Philippines' Statehood USA: 51st State of the United States of America;

Book 3

by

Oscar S. Abejo

DORRANCE
PUBLISHING CO
EST. 1920
PITTSBURGH, PENNSYLVANIA 15238

The contents of this work, including, but not limited to, the accuracy of events, people, and places depicted; opinions expressed; permission to use previously published materials included; and any advice given or actions advocated are solely the responsibility of the author, who assumes all liability for said work and indemnifies the publisher against any claims stemming from publication of the work.

Dorrance Publishing Co
585 Alpha Drive
Suite 103
Pittsburgh, PA 15238
Visit our website at www.dorrancebookstore.com

ISBN: 978-1-6491-6839-9
eISBN: 978-1-6491-3857-6

In Their Memory

I am dedicating this book, to my father Clodualdo O. Abejo, a veteran of WWII. He is now resting in peace at the Libingan ng mga Bayani in Taguig, MM, Philippines and to my uncle Francisco O. Abejo, who died during the Bataan Death-march WWII on April 1942. His body was never found. May he also rest in peace.

I believe that in their small way, minute it maybe, they helped America win the war.

FOREWORD

I am compelled to bring forth this "Philippines' Statehood USA" movement again because of the situation prevailing at hand. I said "again" because this crusade had been launched forty years ago by PAF Ret. Col. Bartolome C. Cabangbang in 1981, but for some reason it fizzled out.

Today after four decades of facing uncertainties, dangers, and hardships, I believe the condition now is ripe for a real and genuine change.

I am writing this book in simple American English without using highfaluting words so everyone will understand what is happening to our country today.

Bear in mind that this movement will not only benefit the Philippines and the United States but the whole world as well because there will be check and balance over at the Pacific and China Seas, which will lead to prosperity, stability, and world peace.

Obviously, China will not like this plan, but they cannot object to this movement because the decision will come only from two countries, the Philippines and the US.

Oscar Salazar Abejo

Lisle, Illinois, May 22,2020

Note Bene (NB):

This is a **Nonfiction** book, and the writings herein are based on facts. And in order to give emphasis to them, I have opted for a one-page presentation so that you beloved readers could write down some notes on these vacant pages, if need be.

Table of Contents

CHAPTER 1

Flashback: Brief History

As we all know, people move around. And as anthropologists would write it, people move around to hunt for food, and as they became more civilized, they move around to barter as well, meaning the exchanging of food for another goods, and this went on and on, until money was invented. Then the word "trade" became more appropriate to use.

Then people moved around to distant places to trade by navigating through rivers and seas. And when the big sailboats were invented (*called galleons—to Portugal's credit*) people moved around crossing oceans.

In 1492 Christopher Columbus was credited for sitting foot in America as to Ferdinand Magellan's discovering the Philippines in 1521. (*Remember though, it is an accepted fact that many traders like the Vikings, Polynesians, Malayans, Chinese had set foot in these places too, but since no records were made on these travels, they could not get any credit for them, and it was not until the voyages commissioned by the kings in the later years that got*

recognized because they had on board their ships recorders to log down their journeys).

Let's rewind a little bit: centuries ago, many nations had commissioned numerous expeditions that led to the discoveries and annexation of many places into their kingdoms and they called them colonies (territories). To name a few of these colonizers, there was Great Britain, Spain, Portugal, the Scandinavian countries, Russia and many more. America isn't included in this list because at that time, the US was just a developing nation.

As common as it is, even today, trade disputes arose and some nations wage war against another, and Spain was commonly involved in most of these wars.

By the end of the 1800s, Spain unfortunately had lost all of its New World* colonies leaving only Cuba and Puerto Rico. https://fcit.ustedu/florida/lessons/s-a war/sa war1.htm (*Early colonial geographers believe that the world was composed only of Africa, Europe, and Asia, and when America was discovered they called it the *New World). Please open website: https://fcit.usf.edu/florida/lessons/s-a war/s-a war1.htm about the Cuban unrest that led to the US-Spanish war.

Probably because of proximity, the trade between Cuba and the US flourished compared to the trade between Cuba and Spain. Many Cubans did not wish to be under Spanish rule, so they asked for independence and this led to unrest. Some Cubans fled to Florida and other parts of the United States. Because the US had some investments in Cuba, it was not surprising for the US's ships to hop in and set sail to Cuba. It was in one of the visits of the *USS Maine* to Cuba when it was sabotaged. The *Maine*, exploded and sank on February 15, 1898. This caused the eruption of war between the US and Spain.

The Spanish-American War, which was waged in the Philippine waters, lasted only for a few months. It ended after Spain signed a peace treaty giving the United States control of Cuba, Puerto Rico, the Philippine islands, and Guam in exchange for $20,000,000. The United States recognized Cuba as an independent nation, but would not agree to withdraw their forces unless the Cubans agreed to several conditions. Cuba ultimately became an independent country rather than a US territory.

Chapter 2

Commonwealth Philippines

I am not going to touch on a conspiracy theory floated around by some parties, saying it was the US themselves who blew up their own ship, a pretext to enable them to wage a sure-win war against a weakling Spain, because this is a baseless theory.

The fact appearing on records is that there was an ongoing unrest in Cuba and the populace was asking for independence from Spain. And because the US being a good trade partner of Cuba who had businesses there in Cuba, and having all the good reasons to visit Cuba to inspect and or protect their investment, somebody blew up their ship. And there was no one to be rightfully blamed but the jealous Spain. Or maybe it could also be floated that since the Cubans knew that the US had superior naval power to Spain, who knows, for it could be the Cubans themselves who secretly initiated this sabotage so the blame could be put on Spain, so their trade partnership with the US would go on unhalted.

But that's all history now. And another chapter is unfolding right in front of our own very eyes. Today, independent Cubans

are not happy with the way their nation is being run by its leaders, who turned into communism.

The Philippines and Cuba, though thousands of miles apart, seem to have an intertwined destiny, for without Cuba's unrest against Spain, which lead to an all-out Spanish-American War, the Philippines would not have been freed from the shackles of Spain. But was that good or bad? Let's have a look and let's compare their similarities and differences.

The Philippines with an area of 115,800 sq. miles lies in Asia, while Cuba having an area of only 42,400 sq. miles lies in what was originally called the New World and they are 9,700 miles apart. Both countries were colonies of Spain. Both countries revolted against Spain. Cuba was granted independence by Spain and was acknowledged by the US after their war in 1898. The Philippines became a commonwealth after that Spanish-American War in 1898 and was granted independence forty-eight years later in 1946. The above facts illustrate the similarities between them.

Unfortunately, they have differences too. The Philippines became an ally of the US during WWII against Japan, but Cuba was not. After gaining its independence, Cuba drifted away, started undermining the US, then became a communist government, became an ally of Russia, and almost ignited a nuclear war against the US in the early 1960s.

Meanwhile the Philippines continued to be an ally of the US even after its independence, although today the Philippines seems to be courting China to the dismay and ire of all the scholars both in the Philippines and the US. The Philippines enjoys billions of US dollars being sent by Filipinos living in the US to their homeland, the Philippines.

The Philippines with an area of 115,800 sq. miles, lies in Asia, while Cuba having an area of only 42,400 sq. miles lies in

what was originally called the New World and they are 9,700 miles apart. Both countries were colonies of Spain. Both countries revolted against Spain. Cuba was granted an independence by Spain and was acknowledged by the US after their war in 1898. The Philippines became a common-wealth after that Spanish-American war in 1898 and was granted an independence forty-eight years later in 1946. The above facts illustrate the similarities between them.

Unfortunately, they have differences too. The Philippines became an ally of the US during WW II against Japan, but Cuba was not. After gaining its independence, Cuba drifted away, started undermining the US, then became a communist government, became an ally of Russia and almost ignited a nuclear war against the US in the early 1960s.

Meanwhile the Philippine continued to be an ally of the US even after its independence, although today the Philippines seems to be courting China to the dismay and ire of all the scholars both in the Philippines and the US. The Philippines enjoys billions of US dollars being sent by Filipinos living in the US to their homeland, the Philippines.

CHAPTER 3

Love and Hate the USA; Brief History of the Philippines

The Philippines' history was quite tumultuous, but it became colorful when some people injected humor into it. Take a look at this saying: 'The Philippines was kept inside the convent for almost 400 years by Spain, then it was let loose inside Hollywood for fifty years by the US, so Filipinos pray while dancing or they know how to dance while praying."

After Magellan discovered the Philippines in 1521, there seems to be not much historic record until 1565. Then from 1565-1898, the Philippines was headed by the Governor Generals initially appointed by the Viceroy in Mexico authorized by Spain. There was, however, a brief period of five years (1761-1764) when the Philippines had two leaders, one stationed in Cavite while the other was stationed in Bacolor, Pampanga. This was the period when Spain lost to Britain but ultimately regained it in 1765. Then appointments for governorship came directly from Spain. Please refer to website written below for details. https://en.wikioedia.orq/wiki/Governor-General of the Philippines

This much-talked-about Spanish-American War was not actually fought in Cuba but in Manila Bay, under Commodore George Dewey. Later he attained the rank of admiral for his phenomenal brilliancy. He was the only officer in US history to receive this honor. He won that battle despite his shortage of fuel and ammunition; and his armada suffered only one loss of life. To honor his feat, the busiest street in Manila was named after him and was called Dewey Boulevard. It stood there for almost 100 years until Marcos changed it to Roxas Boulevard in the 1960s.

The aftermath of the war was quite stormy itself, for while it was being fought, other nations, who had businesses in Manila, had sent their own battleships too. And so Manila Bay was filled with warships of Britain, Germany, France, and Japan. The German fleet of eight ships provocatively bragged its presence, cutting in front of America's ships and ignoring US victory over Spain, even refusing to salute the US flag while landing supplies for the recently defeated Spain, as if challenging the US into another war again. Dewey called Germany's bluff but ultimately Germany called off their offensive display of un-called-for pride.

Meanwhile as news became known throughout the land that the defeated Spain was again building up its military forces in Manila to fight American forces again, the US brought back Aguinaldo from Hong Kong, *(Aguinaldo was exiled to Hong Kong by Spain for instigating revolt. This was before the Spanish-American War had started)*. With Aguinaldo siding with the US, skirmishes with Spain finally ended.

Meantime, over at the new world, a new scenario was unfolding in Cuba. Spain had granted Cuba its independence sanctioned by America. This triggered off a resentment by the

Filipinos who were also equally fighting for its own independence too, the way the Cubans were fighting theirs. (One of the reasons America could not grant independence to the Philippines was, America wanted to have a foothold in Asia to countercheck the military advances that Japan was making in China).

The scenario became more chaotic because right after the defeat of Spain by the combined forces of the Americans and the Filipinos, Aguinaldo declared the Philippines independence on Jun 12, 1898 in Cavite. Then on February 4, 1899 the Filipino-American War begun. This bloody war ended on July 2,1902. Then the commonwealth government of the Philippines was established.

Chapter 4

Nationalism

These series of wars, which the Philippines underwent, had instilled the virtue of nationalism in the minds of the Filipinos. In fact, they are willing to die if someone tramples their sacred shores, as the song goes.

As the Philippines were transitioning into a commonwealth government, the fight for its independence from Ameca was going on too. One of the Philippines' notable and prominent characters was President Manuel Quezon. Quezon was an eloquent speaker of his time. *(probably next to Marcos who was named in his speech to the joint US congress in 1965, as the greatest orator of the five worlds)*. Quezon's speeches had inspired everyone that it became an instant quotation even up to this day. Two of his famous quotes were: 1. "My loyalty to my party ends when my loyalty to my country begins," and (2) I'd rather see my country run like hell by the Filipinos than run like heaven by the Americans." As the Philippines continued to grapple for progress, powerless people cannot help but somehow relate this infamous speech of Quezon to the struggling

state of the country today. Some people would inject some sense of humor into them, saying, "so we finally got what we wished for just to deaden the upsetting effect of being overtaken by some countries who were once behind us."

It's always a common occurrence that, unless your boss owns the property or the company that he is administering, there are always whispers from the people below saying "**I could do better than him**." This is true to a nation too, that unless you are the king, elected heads of states are always under scrutiny by the officers working below them. Unless something is done, these whispers will grow bigger and louder, and soon it will become a protest growing into a rebellion. Their most common reason albeit alibi is "corruption." The Philippines asking for independence from the US was an outcry of the saying, "Filipinos could do it better than its incumbent American leadership," but look what happened now, the Philippines' growth has stalled and worse, it was overtaken by its neighbors who were once lesser-developed than them.

History would tell us that a large majority of nations that were given independence have failed. Chaos and unrest became too common. Take a look at these two websites containing the list of counties that had gained independence and you will see where they are now: https://en.wikipedia.org/wiki/List of countries that have gained independence from the United Kingdom and https://en.wikipedia.org/wiki/List_of sovereign_states by date of formiation

Some of these countries on the list had turned around 180 degrees even becoming an enemy of the group of nations, examples are Afghanistan and Iran.

CHAPTER 5

Acquisition by Negotiation

While in the previous chapters I mentioned to you that most territories were acquired by strong nations by virtue of their winning the war, there were also some that were acquired through negotiations. One notable case is that of Alaska, the biggest state of the United States having a total area of 663,267 square miles.

How did this happen. The facts presented in:

https://en.wikipedia.org/wiki/Russian colonization of the Americas says that during the reign of Peter the great of Russia, which was followed by his wife Empress Catherine, they encouraged their people in expanding towards the east for trading and hunting animals for fur (scalp is to humans as fur is to hairy animals). Because this proved to be a profitable livelihood for the Russians, more people came and settled there in Alaska. Their encroachment, however, had brought tension between themselves and the native Alaskans. Fortunately, or unfortunately, or depending how we look at it, during this period, Russia's economy was on the decline, a ramification brought

about by the Crimean War, and the decision reached by the government of Russia under Emperor Alexander was to sell Alaska to the US. And in October 18, 1867, for a price of $7.2 million, Alaska became a territory of the United States of America.

Comes now this book, which is a movement for making the Philippines a state of the United States. Could this be done? Is this possible? My answer of course is yes, but I am not the deciding factor here. It is the people of the Philippines and the government of the United States of America.

I believe that the most logical way is for the people of the Philippines to be asked whether they want to be part of US or not, and if the answer is affirmative, then they bring their case to the US government for their acceptance, and I believe in a heartbeat they will.

CHAPTER 6

Dignity of Labor is a Perfect Start

Sometime in 1989 while I was in Japan working as a consultant engineer for geothermal production, I talked to our drill-pipe inspector named Rahim, a Singaporean whose father loved the Philippines very much. He did not specify why his father did so, but I guessed one Filipino saved his life during the war. He said, his father hoped for Singapore to copy the development and progress of the Philippines. But Rahim's father was disappointed when his much-admired Philippines was overtaken by Singapore in terms of progress, in terms of infrastructure, in terms of work, employment, income, healthcare, and so on and so forth. He was expecting that the Philippines would still be ahead of them as the two nations have similar climates and governments. "Well, could you ask your father what he thinks the Philippines' problem was?" When we met again, Rahim said, his father believed it's because of our leaders.

During those years that I was in Japan, I learned that our liaison officer Mr. Semana speaks Nihongo very fluently. He said his wife being Japanese taught him the language. They are

now living in Japan. I asked him what it is like living in Japan. He said he loves Japan and he likes the Japanese people. He said, they are honest, well-disciplined, hard-working, and law-abiding citizens who believe in the dignity of labor. He also said, he saw its rapid growth from the time he was there working as a Filipino counterpart in the reparation payment of Japan to the Philippines. It was an impoverished Japan after losing the war, but its comeback growth was so phenomenal that in just three decades it became an industrialized country to be reckoned with.

In 1972 while I was in New Zealand on my post-graduate studies in geothermal subsurface measurements, its Ministry of Works site manager who was also an engineer, was impressed with my working ethics. On one occasion, he confided to me like an elder brother. He said he wished he were like me when he finished college where I was not afraid nor embarrassed to get my hands dirtied from work. He saw me quickly learn and became adept in handling and working with different kinds of tools and instruments. I quickly picked up what he meant: it is a common attitude for college graduates to dress up elegantly and be holed up in the office without knowing the different tasks below him. He believes I could run all kinds of endeavors because I know the trades of geothermal development from top to bottom.

When I returned to the Philippines, I showed the newly hired and fresh graduate engineers how to work with both hands in the field and with a writing pen in the office. I am proud to say that I trained quite a lot of people, who are now good supervisors and managers.

CHAPTER 7

I Like to Be in America

In the early 1960s when I was still a student at MIT Philippines, there was a song very often played on TV broadcast whose lyrics reads: *I like to be in America, okay by me in America. Everything's free in America, for a small fee in America*! I think this was a song created by the famous composer Leonard Bernstein.

On one occasion while walking to school, I passed another fellow student humming that song. I smiled at him and said, "So you like that song very much, huh?" He answered me, "Oh yes, my elder brother is there, working in the pineapple plantation in Hawaii." I thought, maybe one day I could go there too; hopefully it would be easier because my father is a war veteran. At that time my parents were still actively teaching in the public school.

That song however just faded away as an election was coming into play, because more political ads were being broadcast on both radio and television.

After finishing my engineering degree, I became a volcanologist and had worked closely at Taal and Mayan Volcanoes.

We were also trained at the Commission on Volcanology, to work with both hands as well as with our brain, we write reports, operate the seismograph, smoke the paper that was wrapped around the seismograph drum where quakes were recorded, and later we dipped them into a varnish jar to preserve the recorded quakes. I endeavored to learn how to operate a speedboat, a daily routine job to inspect the volcano located about an hour away from our station right in the volcano island itself.

To me this was an improvement from the hand paddling that I did on board a dug-out boat during my elementary-grade years, our house was located by the riverbank enabling us to learn how to swim and paddle dinghies and maneuver boats powered by sails, as early as in my second grade.

I was at ComVol when my post-graduate studies in geothermal subsurface measurements was realized. After my study, it was deemed necessary to transfer to another entity solely devoted to harnessing geothermal power. I became a superintendent at PNO-EDC for quite a time, and it was also here where I earned my second post-graduate schooling, also in New Zealand.

Then there was this regime-change. The further development of the hundreds of megawatts that we developed was halted as the new administration took command of the government. Then a huge opportunity came by way of Japan. A patriotic Japanese businessman named Mr. Uchida (rest in peace, Senses) took notice of the rapid and successful development of the geothermal resources in the Philippines and seeing that the Philippines' program was put on hold, he offered us to work with him in Japan for a much much bigger compensation; we could not refuse.

This Japan journey enabled me to live in a plush village Ayala Alabang. This became my jumping board to relocate and live here in the US where my whole family are now residing.

CHAPTER 8

Mix with Them, Assimilate with Them

I have always thought that the best way to talk to you and hopefully convince you to join me in the platform of Philippine Statehood into the US is to present to you my personal journey. There are ups and downs, but "believe you me," this movement is for the best for all of us, the majority of the world included.

My first job when I reached Los Angeles was in the plastic industry as a manual sorter in the quality control section. My income was augmented by tutoring students, and in other times as a temporary substitute teacher for an elementary algebra class.

To us, the weather in LA doesn't really feel like America for it was more of a copycat of Baguio, temperate-cold but no snow. We know it best because our eldest son was enrolled at the Philippine Military Academy. We thought would it not be nice if we lived in a four-season state, so we moved to the Midwest, and we chose Illinois.

My first job in Illinois was very much connected to my hobby, which was photography. I worked to process mammograms and chest x-ray films. I became interested in the images

coming out from the darkroom and our radiologist Dr. Leaf took notice of my curiosity of them. He somewhat tested me to segregate the ones that I thought needed further tests, and my batting average was a funny 30 percent. As he tutored me further, my score somewhat rose to about 70 percent. I was thinking of going to school to become like him, but the company where I was working was purchased by another bigger competitor and the facility was moved to another area.

Since three of our four children were in the healthcare business, I deemed it wise to study nursing so I could be on the same page with them, (I could have worked in the engineering field, but that would mean weeks of separation from my family). So, I took up the much talked-about C.N.A. short for certified nursing assistant at Triton College, took and passed the state exams and became one of them. Then while working in the Nursing Center. I took a Pharmacy Technician course. Unfortunately, it was not to my liking because the job itself was confined to a small and tight place to move around.

Later, I finally enrolled at the College of Dupage and took up Nursing because I was aiming to become a registered nurse. I liked the class, though I was made to take up biology again, mathematics again, and chemistry again, despite my telling the school that I have already taken these subjects in bachelor's degree years earlier. Long story short, I took them up again because that was the school rules, (college graduates of more than five years needing further education had to repeat taking them).

Funny, but I was even once labeled as the oldest student in America for about a semester. The schooling was good, and most of the time I was in the forefront of debate because I was very much against illegal and undocumented immigration, acts like sneaking through the border. My battle cry was, "I do not

want Juan at the other side of the fence line to change his name to Elvis Presley once he sneaks successfully through the border. I also invoked the humanitarian reasoning to be applied equally to all people in Asia who have to wait and wait for their visa (which sometimes gets disapproved) just so they could reach America.

Unforeseen events do happen: my aging mother passed away, followed by my only sibling, a younger brother, a lawyer, who worked in an immigration law office.

I stopped schooling after those two dark chapters happened. I thought, that at an age of late sixties, why should I not enjoy my retirement, and just help my children in their businesses? At this writing, where I am now in my early seventies, retired, and enjoying my pension, my Medicare, and my almost-free medicines (and please not now) hospitalization as well.

CHAPTER 9

Fulfillment

It's always an agonizing move, if you are in the Philippines to leave your house, either for work or for miscellaneous trips like running errands, going to grocery stores, eating outside with your family, and so forth, because you will surely spend or waste the whole day even just for small chores like the ones above. And, unless of course your destination is a walking distance from where you live, it seems every move we make is always associated with frustration. This is a true occurrence in both metro cities as well as in the rural areas. Vehicular traffic is horrendous in the metropolis while public transport is so scarce in the provinces.

This situation is aggravated by the fact that the cost of living is extremely high. Cost of living should not be confused with standard of living as they are two different things.

Modesty aside, I was also a big shot in the Philippines. I used to be a superintendent of the whole geothermal production of the whole country. People called me "Sir" with respect; we reside in Ayala Alabang; we have cars; children could go to

school at their choice; we could buy food; and yet something was missing. I could not find "fulfillment" in life. And mind you, this word seems illusive to everyone in the Philippines.

Whenever I go out of the village, it will take us so many hours to return home because of heavy traffic. While I reckon I could live all right in the Philippines, a good question of "what about my children, or my grandchildren?" is left unanswered. Would their lives be brighter or gloomier? Life seems to be always on a "survival" mode with endless uncertainties. And this could even worsen once medical emergencies arises.

When scenarios like this appear in my mind, I cannot help but think about the words of Rahim, saying his father believes it's our leaders' fault; or Mr. Semana's observations on the excellent characters of the Japanese that are lacking in us, or the New Zealander's comment about the wrong attitude of the new graduates who wants to work only in the office and not in the field.

Above all this, I must tell you that although I am earning less money here in America than what I use to earn in Japan, it's only here that I found the fulfillment in life. I am sure you will find fulfillment here too once the Philippines becomes part of America.

CHAPTER 10

Answering Our Needs

The basic human instinct in all of us, I mean all of us normal people, is survival. First is food, then shelter which includes clothing, then our needs branch out depending on our culture, religion, and our plans for the future.

Sometime in 1943, an American Psychologist by the name of Abraham Maslow, presented a paper called the Hierarchy of Human Needs. It did not catch much attention at that time because WWII was raging (1939-45), however as peacetime came, many people looked at it as an ideal model for everyone. Take a look at the triangle called The Hierarchy of Human Needs. https://www.psychologytoday.com/us/blog/hide-and-seek/201205/our-hierarchy-needs

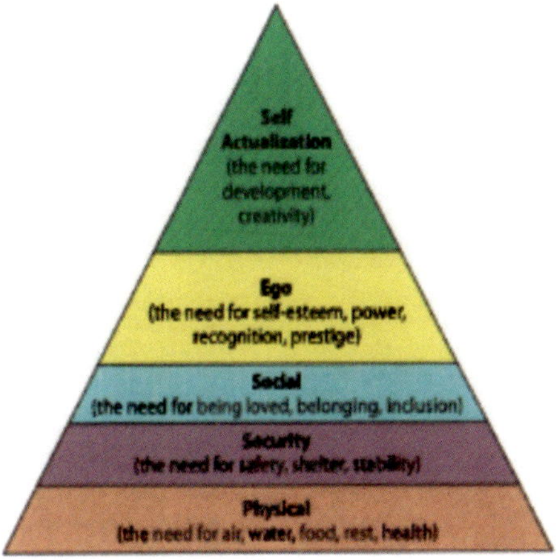

The most common expression you will hear in each of us, middle-class and lower-class people are the words; "make both ends meet." In simple terms, it means, 'budgeting our resources till the next harvest" comes. But what will happen, if after trying everything including working second jobs, selling something just to augment your income, and yet your harvest is not enough; what will you do? The most decent answer is: work overseas.

In the World Bank Report of last year, it said: the United States registered the highest share of overall remittances during the five-month period at 36 percent. Saudi Arabia, Singapore, the United Arab Emirates, the United Kingdom, Japan, Canada, Hong Kong, Qatar, and Kuwait comprised the rest of the top ten sources

https://www.rappler.com/business/236474-overseas-filipino-workers-remittances-january-may-2019

MANILA, Philippines—Migrant workers contributed a huge share in the country's economy in 2018, according to a recent World Bank report.

https://ph.news.yahoo.com/ofw-remittances-4th-biggest-2018-044338960.html_Based on the World Bank's April 2019 Migration and Development Brief, the Philippines received $33.8 billion dollars—the fourth biggest remittance from migrant workers in 2018. India received the biggest remittance with $78.6 billion. followed by China with $67.4 billion, and Mexico's $35.7 billion

From the above data, it can be gleaned if you want to augment your harvest to let your both ends met, then the US is the best place to work. Why, because language is not a problem; the pay is standardized; there is no abuse: and all other goodies exist in the US. For the information of everyone, this is only one of the many benefits that exist in America.

But why work there in the US when you could be in the US yourself without going outside the country? And this could happen once the Philippines becomes a state of the US. Now, what about national security? The US is one of the most if not the most secured nation on earth. The US does not bully anyone, on the contrary, it's the other way around, meaning occasionally you will find some people who go beyond their freedom of speech, which at times they say bad things against the government.

CHAPTER 11

Bullies Around Us

If you type in your computer browser the instructions: define bully, it will say—it is a person who habitually seeks to harm or intimidate those whom they perceive as vulnerable.

I do not want to write other people's character about this subject "bully" because I consider it offensive and unethical, instead, I will devote this paragraph about myself. During the few years of my parent's assignment in the hinterlands of the Philippines to teach the adults how to read and write, (that was after World War II) the house that my parents bought was located by the riverbank. So, I learned how to swim early and to paddle small dug-out boats. Later I developed the enthusiasm of boat racing with boys of my age. When I got into high school, I seemed to have drifted into a group of students who were followers of Steve Reeves, a famous body builder, who played the role of Hercules in the movies. Because we were bigger, stronger, and muscular than the rest of my classmates, nobody dared to touch or intimidate us. And by the time I reached college, I became a fan of Gabriel Flash Elorde, so I enrolled in

boxing and body building at YMCA. So again, nobody touched me for fear of being hurt.

I am a believer of peace and from the illustration above, I can say, that if you are strong, you will be respected and no one will intimidate you. In short, no one but no one will fight against you. There is peace if you show strength. As President Trump said, he wants the US military to be the strongest in the world because "there is peace if you show strength." He said further that he fervently hopes he never has to use it.

Now comes the Philippines. To its north is Taiwan (formerly called Formosa), while on its western side is China. Formosa was a very familiar name in the 1950s because this was the place that Chiang Kai Sheik fled into after his nationalist form of government in China was toppled by the communist Mao Zendong.

This chapter "Bullies around us" could be presented by asking two questions, namely:

1. What country is bullying the Philippines?
   Answer: China.
2. What are you doing about it:
   Answer: Nothing!

Here in the US, most of my friends like Duterte because of this brave and courageous ways of clipping the wings of the people who criticize him. In fact, he is being compared to President Donald Trump who has no qualms of attacking his critics.

However, one member of my wife's family, does not like him because his order to eliminate drug addicts without giving them a second chance was against human rights. I've started having second thoughts too, on my liking of Duterte after he

said, "It's foolish to confront China when you are sure to loss the battle." This was a 180 degrees turnaround when he was earlier asked during his campaign if he is willing to confront China. His powerful answer was: "I have long wanted to become a hero, and this is now my chance to sail and confront the bully."

Today he seems to be submissive and subservient to China's whims and caprices. Why? When things like this happens, I cannot help but look back at his most vocal critic, former Senator Antonio Trillanes, saying that Duterte has a secret bank account containing enormous amounts of gift money. I think Duterte is not corrupt, but when he exhibits his obedience and loyalty to China who has been noted to monetarily reward nations who display unquestionable liking to them, I cannot help but think that maybe there is meat to the claims of former Senator Trillanes that maybe Duterte is accepting rewards from them not necessarily into his pocket but maybe in a form of foreign aids in exchange for being subservient to them.

News flash: April 20, 2020

Quote: On Friday, Filipinos were upset when the Chinese People's Liberation Army stated on their website that Beijing will be setting up two new districts in Paracels and Spratly Islands and will be under the control of Sansha City. The Nansha District will be handling the Spratly Islands, and the areas surrounding it. Its government will hold office on Yongshu Jiao, China's name for Philippine-claimed Fiery Cross (Kagitingan) Reef. On the other hand, it will be the Xisha District's responsibility to supervise Paracel Islands, the Macclesfield Bank, and other nearby areas. In a statement, Vietnam's Foreign Ministry spokeswoman Le Thi Thu Hang said, "The establishment of the so-called Sansha City and related activities seriously violated Vietnam's sovereignty. Vietnam demands that

China respect Vietnam's sovereignty and abolish its wrongful decisions," she added. **Unquote**

For details, see Website: https://www.msn.com/en-ph/news/national/will-the-philippines-remain-submissive-after-china-reveals-plan-to-establish-2-new-districts-in-west-philippine-sea/ar-BB12WeAi?Ii=BBr8Mkn

We have had a lot of blunders in the past on this group of islands starting from the claim of Attorney Tomas Cloma in 1956, which was not followed through; then came our recent victory at the International Court of Justice by the previous administration, but the Duterte administration had just squandered them all.

Claims and counterclaims by nations of the Philippines, Taiwan, Vietnam, China make this group of islands a flashpoint for disputes. Few of these islands already belong to the Philippines but because we do not seem to care about them, a predator is taking them away from us. I have likened China to be like a bird of prey. If the mother hen will not keep watch on her chicks, this predator will swoop on them easily for a meal.

China is a ruthless bully, that is why we must always be on the lookout. Let me refresh again the memory of everyone. China wanted to project themselves as heroes of the seas. They wanted to show a virtue of caring for sea travelers. To camouflage their deceitful plans, they started building a lighthouse on the pretext of helping fishermen and other sea travelers, especially in inclement weather. And because of its noble purpose, nobody had protested. Then that lighthouse that they built was expanded, the surrounding area was massively dredged to enlarge the island and now a formidable military fortress, including military airports now permanently stands seemingly saying with pride, nobody and no one comes near us or else suffer untold consequences.

Last June of 2019, a group of twenty-two Filipino fishermen were rammed over by a Chinese naval ship. https://www.breitbart.com/asia/2019/06/13/philippines-threatens-to-cut-ties-with-china-over-barbaric-south-china-sea-ship-sinking/

All twenty-two of them held to dear life, fortunately after six hours in the sea clinging into their sinking boat, a Vietnamese fisherman passed by and rescued them. But what did the Philippine government do? First they conducted an investigation with a reason that it could have been the fishermen's fault hence their boat was destroyed. Finally because the press was so concerned of the fishermen's welfare, the Philippines finally but hesitantly voiced a protest against China.

I am now a US citizen and I am proud to tell everyone that America respects human lives. If the US Coast Guard will catch someone illegally within the jurisdiction of the US coast, they will never ram their boat, but instead they will apply the full force of the law and bring them all to justice.

CHAPTER 12

China, China, China

If you will ask a baby boomer, or people born after WWII, what their early memories of China were, they will tell you right away, the shelling and bombardment of Quemoy Islands in Formosa. This happened when People's Republic of China's leader Chiang Kai Sheik was forced to flee out of China to Formosa (now named Taiwan), after his ouster by the communist Mao.

Then after about a decade, the word "China Syndrome" came around. This is a movie about a nuclear power plant about to meltdown. But this is not the meat of the story. The equivalent of China Syndrome being talked about after the memories of that movie had faded away, is the passivity of the Chinese government, meaning their willingness to go all the way to see any experiment or any endeavor see its finish line, and who cares if somebody will perish, for after all they have billions of people to spare.

Then, after again another decade, the Tiananmen Square massacre happened in June of 1989. This was about the revolt initiated by Chinese students wanting reforms of their communist

government. And according to the classified report smuggled out of China, https://www.independent.co.uk/news/world/asia/tiananmen-square-massacre-death-toll-secret-cable-british-ambassador-1989-alan-donald-a8126461.html, at least 10,000 people have died.

As I mentioned in Chapter 1, "trade" had always been the most popular channel of contact amongst people and nations, this is where agreements are struck and formulated with one another. But disputes happen too. After World War II, GATT (short for General Agreement for Tariff and Trade) was formed primarily to affect smooth trade relations between nations. On 1 January 1948, GATT entered into force. The twenty-three founding members were: Australia, Belgium, Brazil, Burma, Canada, Ceylon, Chile, China, Cuba, Czechoslovakia, France, India, Lebanon, Luxembourg, Netherlands, New Zealand, Norway, Pakistan, Southern Rhodesia, Syria, South Africa, the United Kingdom, and the United States. Then, amidst this agreement, which the world traders are adhering to, there are complaints that China is making trade strategies to protect themselves. Take a look: https://answers.yahoo.com/question/index:_vlt=ApYk3RLH_RRFoQnCvVpFy0YizKIX;_vlv=3?qid=20071023144824AAfmnX7 *China causes its money to fall to increase the amount of investment in China and to either force out of business, or are forced to give up their patriotism to the US and hire foreign workers in China.*

America can compete with other countries but China. America is near the top of the list in workers productivity. It even outranks Japan, India, China, and almost all of Europe, etc. However, America and the European Union cannot compete against countries that artificially devalue their currencies just to decrease the prices of their products, thus killing the Western nations. Make its exports cheap to America. This creates a situation where American employers cannot

compete against China. Because of their inability to compete, employers will close shop and transfer somewhere else, and the best place to put their business is China. Allowing the trade deficit growth to continue will create an unsustainable condition where trillions of dollars of the GDP are transferred other countries. That causes a lowering of the standard of living, and increases personal debt, slower wage growth, an increase in government debt. News flash: https://michaelpillsbury.net/recap-of-michael-pillsburys-excellent-cpac-speech-on-china/

https://en.wikipedia.org/wiki/Michael Pillsbury

https://thehundredyearmarathon.com/

Michael Pillsbury, a renowned scholar who speaks fluent Mandarin and had devoted much of his life carefully studying the hidden strategy adopted by China, wrote in his book *The Hundred-year Marathon*, that the Chinese view America and its leaders—as barbarians who will be the architects of their own demise. Pillsbury also explains how the US government has helped—sometimes unwittingly and sometimes deliberately—to make this "China Dream" come true, and he calls for the United States to implement a new, more competitive strategy toward China as it really is, and not as we might wish it to be. *The Hundred-year Marathon* is a wake-up call as we face the greatest national security challenge of the twenty-first century. https://www.msn.com/en-us/news/world/china-is-leasing-an-entire-pacific-isiand-its-residents-are-shocked/ar-AAIRg4z?Ii=BBnb7Kz&ocid=msn360

China expanding secretly to take control of the world. China is leasing an entire Pacific island. Its residents are shocked. By Damien Cave Oct 17, 2019

SYDNEY, Australia—The island of Tulagi served as a South Pacific headquarters for Britain then Japan, and during World War

II, its natural Deepwater Harbor made it a military gem, Now, China is moving in with plans to effectively take control.

Under a secretive deal signed last month with a provincial government in the Solomon Islands, a Beijing-based company with close ties to the Chinese Communist Party has secured exclusive development rights for the entire island of Tulagi and its surroundings.

The lease agreement has shocked Tulagi residents and alarmed American officials who see the island chains of the South Pacific as crucial to keeping China in check and protecting important sea routes. It is the latest example of China using promises of prosperity to pursue its global aspirations—often by funneling money to governments and investing in local infrastructure projects that critics call debt traps for developing nations.

"The geography tells you that this is a good location," said Anne-Marie Brady, a China scholar at the University of Canterbury in Christchurch, New Zealand. "China is expanding its military assets into the South Pacific and is looking for friendly ports and friendly airfields just like other rising powers before them."

Beijing's ambitions in the South Pacific have economic, political and military ramifications, and the world must know about this, so that at the end, we should work together to stop China's rampage.

CHAPTER 13

China is Buying the World

I want to devote this whole chapter to show to you the acquisition of the world's giant companies that have now been under china's ownership and or having China as the major owner. These companies are:

1. HNA bought Irish aircraft leasing company Avolon: $5.2 billion (£4.2bn)
2. CNPC bought a stake in a Kazakhstani oil and gas company: $5.3 billion (£4.2bn)
3. Haier bought General Electric's appliance division: $5.4 billion (£4.3bn)
4. CNPC bought a stake in Iraq's Rumaila oilfield: $5.6 billion (£4.5bn)
5. ICBC bought a stake in South Africa's Standard Bank: $5.6 billion (£4.5bn)
6. Anbang bought American company Strategic Hotels & Resorts: $5.7 billion (£4.6bn)

7. CEEC, PowerChina and Sinopec's invested in Nigeria's Mambilla Power Station: $5.8 billion (£4.6bn)
8. COSCO invested in Greek port Piraeus: $5.8 billion (£4.6bn)
9. CGN bought Malaysian energy company Edra: $6 billion (£4.8bn)
10. HNA bought American computer parts distributor Ingram Micro: $6 billion (f4.8bn)
11. HNA also bought a stake in Hilton Worldwide: $6.5 billion (f5.2bn)
12. China Minmetals, Suzhou Guoxin and CITIC bought Peru's Las Bambas copper mine: $7 b(f5.6bn)
13. Shuanghui bought American pork company Smithfield Foods: $7.1 billion (f5.7bn)
14. Sinopec bought a stake in Spanish energy company Repsol's Brazilian unit $7.1 billion (f5.7bn)
15. Sinopec also bought Swiss-owned oil co. Addax Petroleum: $7.2 b (£5.8bn) oil producers in West Africa.
16. ChemChina and SAFE bought Italian tire company Pirelli: $7.9 billion (f6.3bn)
17. Tencent bought a majority stake in Finnish games developer Supercell: $8.6 billion (f6.9bn)
18. Geely bought a stake in German carmaker Daimler: $9 billion (E7.2bn)
19. Vanke, Hopu, Hillhouse and Bank of China bought a major stake in Singaporean Warehouse co GLP: $9.1b (L7.3m)
20. Ping An bought a stake in global bank HSBC: $9.7 billion (E7.8bn)
21. HNA bought American company CIT Group's aircraft leasing business: 21410.4 billion (E8.3bn)

22. Chinalco bought a stake in mining giant Rio Tinto: $12.8 billion (E10.3bn)
23. CIC bought pan-European warehouse company Logicoc $13.8 billion (E11.2bn)
24. ChemChina and China Reform Holdings bought Swiss agrochemicals and seed co.Syngenta: $43 b (f34.5b) 25.CNOOC bought Canadian oil and gas company Nexen: $15.1 billion (f12.1bn)

For details visit website: https://www.msn.com/en-ph/money/markets/how-china-is-buying-up-the-world/ss-AAFEuVd?Ii=BBr8Mkn#image=1

On top of this, China has secured a long-period lease of Tulagi Island from the Solomon Islands administrator to develop the area for both commercial and military use *(see previous* **chapter).**

Chapter 14

Fear vs Love

During my early years in college, we had a subject on Humanities, which touched on Marcus Aurelius and Machiavelli. Marcus Aurelius was a Roman emperor from 161 to 180CE and a Stoic philosopher. He was the last of the rulers known as the Five Good Emperors of Rome, the previous four rulers being Antoninus Pius, Hadrian, Trajan and Nerva. As the story goes, when Marcus died, he appeared before the Gods for judgment. When asked to introduce himself and relate what he had done, he said: "I Marcus Aurelius, a humble philosopher cherish the ambition not to give pain to one another." His words echoed amongst the Gods who chose him to be the best. He also said, he who lives in harmony with himself, lives in harmony with the universe. It was believed that he ruled Rome with love.

On the other side of the spectrum is Niccolo Machiavelli an Italian diplomat of the sixteenth century, a politician, historian philosopher, writer and poet of the renaissance period. He was said to believed that it is 'better to be feared than to be loved if you cannot be both."

I have read the analysis of many people about the "pros and cons" on this virtue, and all of them had good points to raise. However, at the end, I believe that all of us must endeavor to be both, meaning we should be loved and also be feared. Take a look at the good points discussed by a person named Dan and a woman named Kaj Sotala. http://www.sebastianmarshall.com/why-machiavelli-thinks-its-better-to-be-feared-than-loved

In the words of Dan, he said: "In my experience, the mixture of love and fear is called "respect"—that's exactly what you describe as "being loved (admired, looked up to, etc.) and with a speck of fear in the background, and it's definitely the most effective thing, but difficult to achieve."

On the other hand, Kaj Sotala has also a very interesting point, take a look: "The thought occurred to me that this is basically what most parents are. Kids love their parents, but also fear the punishment they'll get if they don't behave. And as kids become teenagers, the parents' ability to apply fear weakens, and the kids typically obey their parents less."

CHAPTER 15

Why is the Philippines' Progress So Slow?

Three of our four children are with the Healthcare Industry (the fourth one is now with commercial aviation flying the big birds) and I am assisting them by driving the wheelchair van to service their patients as they go about with their needs. Occasionally, whenever I drive their staff nurses, CNAS to their respective patients, I ask them "why the Philippines; progress is so slow"; their answers have some similarities, please take a look;

1. Overpopulation—All of them blames the Catholic Church for opposing the governments population control program.
2. Corruption—I agree.
3. Too many Islands—Yes, I do agree with them too.
4. Humid Weather—No, I do not agree with them
5. Nepotism—Yes, I do agree with them.
6. Too many cooks spoil the broth- I am silent in this issue.
7. Too many educated people, most are lazy—Yes, I do agree

8. Too much politics—Yes, I do agree with them
9. Asking for independence too early— Yes. I do agree
10. Location, being visited by Typhoon many times a year—I disagree with them because Japan, Hong Kong, Singapore, Taiwan are visited by typhoons quite often too and yet they are so progressive.
11. Culture: there are scholars who have an equally important analysis. James Fellows in his article to the Atlantic Journal, said "Culture" is another factor for the slow-foot progress of the Philippines. In his article titled "Damaged Culture" where he compared the Philippines to its neighbors, he observed some concerning habits of us Filipinos which are detrimental to our society. He said, we pride ourselves on our lifelong loyalty to the family, schoolmates, compadres, residents of same barangay, and this means total devotion only to within the circle, and total war on those who are outside of it. And because the boundaries of decent treatment is limited to with in the family clan only, the remaining chunk of about 90 percent of the population suffers. Filipinos also fail to care about any public goods, they throw their food wrappers into the street and refuse to cooperate many ways to benefit the public or society. He went further to say, quote: The countries that surround the Philippines have become the world's most famous showcases for the impact of culture on economic development. Japan, Korea, Taiwan, Hong Kong, Singapore—all are short on natural resources, but all have clawed their way up through hard study and hard work. Unfortunately for its people, the Philippines illustrates the contrary: that culture can make a naturally rich country poor. Unquote

12. According to Ravi Zacharias, a renowned religious apologist, there are three religious cultures, namely: Theonomous, Heteronomous, and Autonomous.

Theonomous culture can be found in India. Theos meaning God and nomos meaning law. This culture believes that God's law is within the human heart. It is in you that the consensus in society dwells. Heteronomous culture can be found in the Middle East. Heteros meaning different and there are two distinct sets of operations. The controlling few which is at the top and the followers which are the masses. Marxism and Islam belong to the heteronomous culture. The religious law comes from the top and dictated to the masses to obey whether you want it or not. Meanwhile Autonomous culture can be found in the Western society like America, where we agree to disagree. And we respect people who disagree with us.

In my travels abroad, I've observed that religion, wherever you belong seems to be inversely proportional to the progress of a nation. People in poor nations go to their church, temple, or mosque quite more often than people in progressive countries. While I was working in Japan in their geothermal exploration program, one of our office staff brought me to one of their temples. Because we were busy in the drilling rig, what he did was just bow his head, clap his hands twice, drop coins into the collection box, rang the bell twice, bow our heads again, and then we left the temple and returned back to the drilling operation.

CHAPTER 16

The Bad Things in Both of Us

You probably know what I am getting at, that while we could all be good, there are always a few ugly things here and there that we may not be aware of, and yet we continue to do them. I will not, however, touch politics because in my experience, politicians seem to be the same the world over in the way they carry out their political tasks. I will limit my list of inappropriate actions to two each; thus:

(1) Here in the US: In grocery stores in the likes of Walmart, Meijer, Jewel Osco, and many others where the parking lots are so large; you will observe that more often than not, you will see able-bodied people who just park their vehicles in areas marked for handicap only ignoring the signage. And who are these people? Well, most of them are the minorities.

(2) Here in the US: As common it is everywhere, when you shop, you use a shopping cart to put your goodies into it, after which you head to the cashier's table to pay for

the items that you've gathered, then you go down to the parking lot to unload your purchased goods into your car, and finally you wheel your cart into the corral where all empty carts are finally kept. Unfortunately, most of the time. shoppers just leave these empty carts right by the side of their cars. If you are keen enough, you will notice that most of the people who do these things are shoppers coming from the third world countries. Sad to say, you will also see Filipinos doing this.

(1) There in the Philippines: I was in Manila last May 16, 2019 finishing my book *Inside the Internet Scam*. After checking in at my Airbnb unit, I went out to buy some groceries. Then as I went out of the store going towards the pharmacy to buy some vitamins, a car whom I thought was just going into the parking lot, literally pulled up right in front of me, to unload a passenger. The stop was so abrupt that my dangling groceries in the plastic bag almost hit the car. I stopped because the car had practically blocked my pathway. I waited and waited for about three minutes for the car to move away. but it didn't so I shook my head in disbelief and to my dismay the driver rolled down his window and asked if I have any complain against him. I said, "You are so rude and a discourteous driver; why did you block me?" "Why, who are you?" he asked me sarcastically. "I am an ordinary man just like you, but I know how to respect people, I could report you to the police!" He said, "I am dropping off a senior citizen." I answered back, "But I'm a senior citizen too!" We argued almost to a fistfight, but his mother who had just alighted from his car approached me and pleaded to forgive her son.

(2) There is one thing in us Filipinos that needs to change. I am talking of garbage disposal, garbage segregation and collection. Take a look at this common scene; a couple of individuals are talking on a sidewalk and suddenly a wisp of wind blew by. Then a Styrofoam cup, carried by that gust of wind, stopped right in front of them. Will they pick that trash up or will they just ignore it? Almost all of us will simply ignore it and let the wind carry it farther. In my travels abroad, I have observed that this is also a common behavior in peoples of not-so-rich nations. So maybe this is not only inherent to us but to other third-world nations as well, because here in the US even old people like me will surely endeavor to pick up that floating dirt and toss it into a trash can.

Four decades ago, there was a talented writer from *Atlantic Journal* named James Fallows (*rest in peace James*) who purposely went to the Philippines to observe the Filipino Culture. His article titled "Damaged Culture" was dated 1987, so I guessed he came to Manila as Cory Aquino was being seated as the new President. He mentioned about Smokey Mountain; our over-practice of kinship mentality; and the so-called debt of gratitude virtue and many more. Some people said that feel slighted about what the author wrote, so in case you get hold of this article, I advise you to read it objectively. For more details, please visit: http://www.theattlantic.com/magazine/archive/ 1987/ ll/a-damaged-cullure/505178/ and http://whynationsfail.com/ blog/2012/12/13/a-damaged-culture html

I am sure that once this "statehood USA movement" will succeed, such shortcomings in our culture will be corrected and

fade away. Think of the days of the 'old Hawaii' during the time of Queen Uliuokalani, the last sovereign ruler of Hawaii, which to my research had some similarities with the Filipino's culture; but look at the modern Hawaii today; it is now a state to be proud of.

CHAPTER 17

Kinship Mentality Is a Hindrance to Assimilation

I want to present here, my unforgettable encounter with people coming from one nation whom I believed has not attained yet its age of maturity. Less than a decade ago, I went to Menards Hardware Store in Bolingbrook, Illinois. After I parked my car and started walking towards the main door of the store, I saw an old man (much older than me) aiming to park his car into a vacant slot one lane across from me.

Unfortunately, a younger shopper who drove his vehicle the wrong way beat him to the punch and parked his van into that vacant space the old man was aiming for. So, this poor old guy had no recourse but just to park his car very much far away from the store. Seeing that he walked in pain because of his wobbly gait despite his usage of a quad cane, I confronted this guy and told him that what he did was wrong. He answered me "no English" then he spoke to his three companions who were waiting for him inside the store.

Immediately a big old woman came acting to hit me. I escaped her blow an inch away forcing me to report the matter

to a saleslady whose nameplate reads Maria. I asked Maria to call the police. While we waited for the police to come, Maria approached my assailant and immediately all of them spoke in Spanish. And as I was telling my version of the incident, two policemen arrived. Maria immediately spoke to the police officers and all of them, my assailant included, talked in Spanish. Then one police officer came to me saying, why had I started the fight.

I told the police officer it was them who started the fight and it was me who requested the store lady to summon for a police officer because that woman almost hit my face. I explained to them what happened, but the police officer just ignored my story and worse he said, "If I don't leave the store, they will literally throw me out." The police spoke to me in foul language in favor of their fellowmen. Long story short, we parted ways with the problem being left unsolved. When I arrived home, I jotted down the incident in details for future reference. unfortunately, I lost my notebook when we renovated our house. The most notable marker of time was it happened during the year of the Drew Peterson scandal, a thing I could not forget because both cases involved Bolingbrook policemen.

I blamed myself for not going straight to the police station to report the incident, but on second thought the incident happened after office hours, so nobody will investigate us properly at the police station but only the officer on duty manning the desk.

CHAPTER 18

Philippines' Maturity Getting Noticed

Maybe it's the famous hospitality culture of every Filipinos that molded us into a fair-minded people. Let me cite to you a classical example of fairness and maturity. In 1992, the Philippine's Little League baseball team made headlines after they won the world's championship title. The merrymaking however was short-lived because one Filipino newsman discovered that the team coach allowed a couple of players in their team who technically should be outed. Apparently, one player lived outside the city limits while the other guy turned overage just a day before the start of the tournament. And so, the world baseball association stripped the Philippine's of their coveted world title and their trophy was given to the Long Beach California baseball team.

An ethical question could be asked: what would have happened if that world title was won by another country, say, Mexico or Iran for that matter? Would their own countrymen report this trivial error to the sports body? Well, my answer is as good as yours, they will surely cover that negligible and excusable mistake. (www.nytimes.com/1992/09/18/sports/basebal

Sep 18. 1992 • Little League baseball stripped the Philippines of this year's world series title last night and awarded the championship to Long Beach, California:, saying the Asian team has ineligible players.) Was that news reporter in question a traitor? Immature nations will say yes, he was a traitor, but if you have adopted the culture of fairness in the US, then that newsman was a hero.

CHAPTER 19

Spratly Islands Is a Flashpoint

Presently, there are six claimants of the Spratlys group of islands; they are (1) Philippines (2) China (3) Malaysia (4) Vietnam (5) Brunei (6) Taiwan. Others sources however reports nine claimants (Thailand, Cambodia, Indonesia). China declares all these islands belong to them since "time immemorial," meaning beyond memory on record or since historic times.

Everyone knows that China wants to dominate the world. It is very much envious of the United States. Its recent strategy was to erect a lighthouse at the Spratly Islands in the guise of helping fishermen in distress. But on the contrary, that lighthouse pretext has turned out to be a major naval base construction. They dredged the area and built an airport. Then they installed all the necessary naval warfare equipment, and if nobody will do the checking, I won't be surprised if one morning, the Philippine will wake up to find out that there is already a nuclear missile facility in that area. This reminds me of that US naval blockade against Russia in the 1960s for their putting up of a nuclear missile facility in Cuba targeting mainland USA.

Baby boomers should remember that famous LORAN Station or Long Range Aid for Navigation stations installed by the United States after WWII. It has a noble purpose of genuinely helping the navigators. If I remember them correctly, a LORAN station is composed of a radio set, a lighthouse and a small quarters to shelter its operators. There is one LORAN station in Batanes area, one in Catanduanes, and one in Talampulan (an Island between Mindoro and Palawan). They are there to aid navigators and it does not have naval ships to ram or destroy fishing boats. (*see map – next page*)

Spratly Islands is a flashpoint

As I have written in Chapter 9, a Philippine fishing boat of twenty-two men was purposely rammed over and destroyed by a Chinese Naval vessel last year 2019 while fishing in the Spratly areas. Thanks to a passing Vietnamese boat who rescued them to safety.

This condemnable and barbaric action clearly contradicts China's propaganda of helping fishermen in distress, because on the contrary they are the ones causing distress to navigators. Questions arose immediately after the ramming incident, as to why the Philippines did not even file an international protest against China. On the contrary, what they instead did, was to announce to the press that they will first conduct an investigation for who knows that it could probably had been the fishermen's fault that was why they were rammed over by China's naval ships.

In another similar encounter, a Vietnamese fishing boat became another victim of China's ramming tactics, but Vietnam filed a protest immediately. Please refer to:

https://www.reuters.com/article/us-china-seas-fishermen-idUSBREA4603C20140507

and

https://www.msn.com/en-phinews/world/us-accuses-beijing-of-using-coronavirus-as-cover-for-south-china-sea-activity/ar-BB12gkEp?ll=BBr8Mkn

Above all these, it looks like, it is only Vietnam who has the guts and courage to protest against China without fear. There are six nations that have overlapping claims on the Spratly Islands; the Philippines, China, Malaysia, Vietnam, Brunei and Taiwan and without the US's coming in, this could very well be a starting point for a major conflict. Would it not be nice and peaceful if these Spratly Islands group would be divided fairly and peacefully amongst its claimants in a way similar to the Virgin Islands group in the Caribbean area where the US and the UK are coexisting harmoniously? This maybe a long shot though, because the claimants are of different kinds of government, the democratic and the communists, but again who knows? This could be a good test for mature nations just for the sake of attaining peace in the region. What I fear, though, and I hope I am wrong, that if history is to be visited, conflicts of this kind could only be resolved after an arm confrontation happens, then treaties are discussed on a conference table where offers and counter offers happen.

A valid question could now be asked, what would have happened if the US Naval Base (*Home of the 7th Fleet—se map on page 61*) was not driven away by the Philippine Government? The Philippines drove them away because we believe we could stand on our own feet. And additionally, we also wanted to appease the communist party who constantly make rallies against the Philippines for being a puppet of the US. Our question now

is, were the communist party able to protect the Philippines from China? Or are they the propaganda machinery of China. *Note: Maps came from website -written @ last page marked acknowledgement*

Warning: At this point, it looks difficult to reverse the situation now, because we can no longer go back to the time when the International Court of Justice had just rendered their verdict confirming the claims of the Philippines at the Spratly. The Philippines should have followed this through, but instead we slept on it.

There is however a glimmer of hope, and I am talking of two scenarios to hopefully happen, and they are: one: for the people of Hongkong to win their protest to reform the Chinese Communist government; this is a however a wishful thinking because their leader Martin Lee is already eighty-two years old. Will Martin Lee at his age be able to continue leading a protest? and two: for the Philippines to become a state of the United States of America.

Each one is independent from the other, but both will bring positive change to China for the betterment of the world. Therefore, whoever initiates the movement of Philippines' Statehood to the US, we must all go for it because this is for the best interest of everyone.

CHAPTER 20

Debt of Gratitude

I am writing these first few sentences in bold letters to emphasize to everyone that this D.O.G virtue doesn't seem to exist or has no meaning in China's government. Or is this really the dogma of communism? Have they forgotten and lost track of time that it was the United States who brought them into the light of day?

Three decades ago, China was a cloistered nation, its economic growth was stalled because its products were just circulating around their country. It needed a strong hand to introduce them (China) into the world.

Now comes the United States whose ever-ready attitude of helping people caught sight of China who has no friendly relationship yet with any countries across the pacific until Richard Nixon visited them in February of 1972 to open diplomatic relationship. This was followed by Gerald Ford in 1975. Then Ronal Reagan in 1984, followed by G.H. W. Bush February 1989. Then there was silence because of the Tiananmen Square killings which led to sanctions imposed on them. After this, Bill

Clinton went there in 1998, followed by G.W. Bush in 2001, Barack Obama in 2009 and recently, by President Donald Trump in 2017. Seven US Presidents already visited them as of April 2020.

It was Bill Clinton's ten-days visit to China, the longest by any US President, who pluck China from stagnation by introducing them to the world. Clinton rallied behind China for its membership into the WTO or World Trade Organization From there on, their economy immediately soared high topping other nations to become number one.

It took a billionaire businessman in the person of Donald Trump to discover that China was manipulating their currencies to the disadvantage of the US and other nations. The manipulation was so well-planned that other business establishment in the US transferred to China Millions of jobs were lost because of China unscrupulous business strategies.

Before Clinton completed his two terms of office in the year 2000, he wanted to plant a legacy that it was his administration who made China be a member of WTO, and he did. Not all though thought it was a good idea, the United Auto makers opposed this plan as well as the 197 members of congress. Nevertheless, with a vote of 237 in favor and 197 against it (1 abstained) the bill was passed.

Some quarters however believed that the reason Clinton pursued strongly in getting China into WTO was to equalize the red mark he got after being impeached by congress.

Others however have darker interpretations and they believed differently. Investigative reporters Reed Irvine and Cliff Kincaid (NYTimes January 22, 2003) said Clinton authorized the release of highly classified aerospace documents to China apparently to reciprocate one company named Loral who do-

nated money to the Democratic Party. Although Loral was penalized by millions of dollars of fines, the harm had already been done. For details, refer to website at acknowledgment page.

It is believed that the release of these classified aerospace documents during the Clinton years enabled China improved their rocket launches where before most of them were failures right at their launch pads. Now, it was reported they have developed long range shots even capable of reaching the US which means Taiwan, Philippines, Vietnam etcetera are easy targets.

China does not have "debt of gratitude" to the US for without the help of America, they would not have been a nation to be reckoned that they are today.

I am not trying to blame Bill Clinton for this belligerent attitude of China today, because if it was not him, probably someone else would because this is a plus point in their presidential record.

The problem now is, nobody in the communist party of the Chinese government recognizes this noble act that the US gave to China.

CHAPTER 21

Carrot and Stick Policy of China — Duterte Is Riding High

During my student's days at MIT Philippines. one of my roommates was a guy named Froilan Villaluz. He bragged to us in our dormitory that he mediated two notoriously warring gangsters into a talking-mood. asked him, "how did you do that?" He said he did it over five cases of beer. First, he befriended the leader of one group, then later he again befriended the leader of the other group. And finally, without telling each leader of his plan, he invited each one of them to his birthday party. He boasted and said; "so, if ever I have a problem, I could approach either of them for assistance."

In this Asian-Pacific part of the world, there are two prominent players aiming for leadership, the US and China. China's policy follows the dogma of the "carrot and stick" management, that is combining reward and punishment in order to get their desired goal. The US on the other hand plays like a parent, giving freedom to their children who are above eighteen years of age.

And now here comes a clever Duterte. During his political campaign for presidency, he prided himself after being asked if he is willing to confront China; and he said, "yes, very much so" adding that he has long been wanting to become a hero, and further implying that this is now his chance to do so. And yes, he is very much willing to sail into this group of islands just to confront China's armament. After he was elected president, his promise had changed and faded away, changing it to another clever answer of "why fight a battle when you are sure to loss?" Again, this is another brilliant answer, for indeed, it's impossible nowadays to find a kamikaze fighter unless you are a terrorist willing to blow your own body just to be in heaven.

The problem now is, what shall we do with the child that they abducted from your family which up to now they have not released her yet, despite your befriending them? The child I am talking about is the island in the Spratly group which the international Court of Justice had awarded back to the Philippines eight years ago; under the previous administration.

I believe aiming for a double friendship maneuver, similar to what Froilan Villaluz did, befriending them so he could ask goodies from China and later from another friend whose name is America, is not a productive strategy at all because China have not freed yet the child that they have abducted.

This is a big, big dilemma which the so-called clever strategy can never solve. Meantime, there is a new David in the persona of Vietnam who is not afraid to challenge a Goliath in the person of China.

The latest news as up this day April 9 of 2020 is that the Philippines declared support to the Vietnamese fishermen similarly rammed by the Chinese Naval Ships while fishing within the Spratly islands. Take a look:

https://www.msn.com/en-ph/news/nationa/philippines-calls-out-china-on-rammінq-of-viethamese-vessel/ar-BB12ji,A2?li=BBr8Mkn

In a rare criticism of China, the Philippines on Wednesday decried the sinking of a Vietnamese vessel by the Chinese coast guard off the South China Sea, calling it a "provocative" act that undermines peace and security in the disputed waters. The Department of Foreign Affairs (DFA) issued a "statement of solidarity" in response the incident wherein a Vietnamese fishing vessel, with eight fishermen on board, was rammed and sunk by the Chinese vessel on April 2.

This is a good start voicing out our concern over China's provocative and bullying actions. But for how long would we wait? Shall we wait until Duterte's term is over and new strategy is implemented by the next administration?

Meantime China is continuously building up their naval base. Do you think we can see a light of day when the Spratly claimants could coexist with each other, the way the Caribbean's Virgin Islands inhabitants do? I'm talking of the US who owns about half of the Islands, Islet and cays as well as Britain, who owns the other half.

CHAPTER 22

Oil, Oil, Oil

I am probably the best living witness of how the lighting energy evolved in the Philippines. After WWII, my parents were assigned into the boondocks to teach adult people how to read and write. I saw and I have lived the way the rural folks do. I remember how we extract oil from coconuts and use them to fuel lamps at night, and also use them for frying food. Later as my parents got their promotion and transferred into town, our night lamp was the famous petromax that uses kerosene pumped into a burning filament.

Petromax

I believe this was also the same evolution that happened in some rural areas around the world because when I started traveling abroad and comparing notes with some other baby boomers, my story was like theirs too; the only difference was that their oil did not from coconuts trees but from different sources.

The war machinery however was quite different, for it already utilized the early discoveries of science like using diesel fuel, gasoline and other derivatives from crude oil.

Crude oil, the fluid that comes from beneath the earth has enhanced the lives of each and every one of us. History reveals that this seem to have been used in some parts of the world in the earliest of times though, in other forms of course.

Records show that crude oil was discovered in 1875 in Pennsylvania, USA through the use of drilling rigs and a few years later in 1908 the middle east oil discovery happened. In 1973 when the Middle Eastern countries learned how important crude oil was to the lives of people in the world, they used it as a new weapon to put the world hostage to this product. The word OPEC (organization of petroleum exporting countries) became an expression that scares everyone.

But who are really the biggest producers of oil today and how much are their reserves?

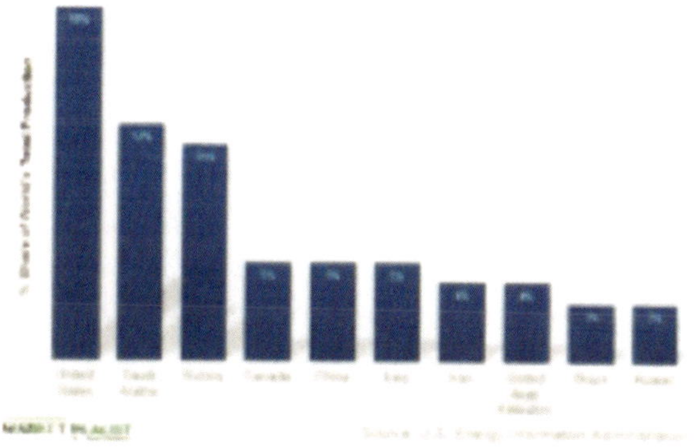

Top 10 Oil Producers in figures

Country	Oil Production	Per Capita
1st USA	15,043,000bbl/d	10,798 bbl/million people
2nd Saudi Arabia (OPEC)	12,000,000	35,922
3rd Russia	10,800,000	73,292
4th Iraq (OPEC)	04,451,516	119,664
5th Iran (OPEC)	03,990,956	49,714
6th China	03,980,650	02,836
7th Canada	03,662,694	100,931
8th UAE (OPEC)	03,106,077	335,103
9th Kuwait (OPEC)	02,903,825	721,575
10th Brazil	02,515,459	012,113

(Note: Phil is 67th at 20 million barrels per day. Place see acknowledgement on page 58)

Top 15 Nations with their corresponding estimated reserves

Country	Oil Reserves	Population by 2020
1st Venezuela	300.90 Billion	0,028,435,940
2nd Saudi Arabia	266.50 Bn	0,934,813,871
3rd Canada	169.70 Bn	0,037,742,154
4th Iran	158.49 Bn	0,083,992,949
5th Iraq	142.50 Bn	0,040,222,493
6th Kuwait	101.50 Bn	0,004,270,571
7th United Arab Emirates	97.70 Bn	0,009,890,402
8th Russia	80.00 Bn	0,145,934,462
9th Libya	48.40 Bn	0,006,871,292
10th Nigeria	37.10 Bn	0,206,139,589
11th USA	36.50 Bn	0,331,002,651
12th Kazakhstan	30.00 Bn	0,018,776,707
13th China	26.60 Bn	1,439,323,776
14th Qatar	25.20 Bn	0,002,881,953
15th Brazil	12.70 Bn	0,212,559,417

How much oil does a person consume per day? According to studies, each person here in the US, consumes about 2 to 2.5 gallons of crude oil per day or https://oilprice.com/Energy/Crude-Oil/How-Much-Crude-Oil-Do-You-Consume-On-A-Daily-Basis.html or twenty-two barrels per year.

And what are the products that comes out from this black gold, a terminology some people use to designate crude oil? There are about ten of them; we have gasoline, diesel, alcohol, lubricating oil, kerosene, industrial solvents, gas, naphtha, and many more.

The Philippines has some oil wells down at the Palawan-Spratly areas, and it is believed or rather estimated to contain about 26.3T of oil deposits. If this is true, then the Philippines is sitting on a pot of gold. But could we exploit that area or much less could we conduct a thorough exploration at the Spratlys? The way the Philippines is showing its cowardice towards China, the answer is "no."

Suppose China exploits that area, could the Philippines say a word, or file a protest? Again, the answer is "No." My wife jokingly said that had this been a "yes or no" exam everyone will surely get a perfect score if he chooses 'no' all throughout the whole quiz.

News Flash as of April19.2020: This disturbing news is headlined: "US says China should stop 'bullying behavior' in South China Sea." Apart from this hostile behavior, a worrisome development is happening over at the Spratly islands. Spotted days earlier was China's ship Halyang Dizhi 8 tagging Malaysia's Oil Exploration Vessel by Petronas to conduct oil exploration studies in that areas. For more details, see website: https://www.msn.com/en-ph/news/world/us-says-china-should-stop-bullying-behaviour-in-south-china-sea/ar- BB12QnR?li=BBr8Mkn

From 1976 up to 1991, I have been involved in drilling operations, both in the Philippines as well as in Japan. The drilling rig we were using is nothing different from the ones being used in oil drilling. The deepest geothermal well we drilled was 12,900 ft. A few were vertical wells but the rest were directionally drilled. We resorted to directional drilling to minimize surface destruction, like cutting down stress and other similar ground works.

Thirty years from my time, drilling technology has advanced and a bully China could use this directional technology to their advantage. With the overlapping claims of six countries over at the Spratlys, directional wells could easily sneak into your claim and sip out your crude oil deposit. This could very well happen knowing very well of China's cleverness.

CHAPTER 23

Wake Up Philippines! Please, Please Wake Up!

Last April 20, 2020 a concerning news from msn.com/en-ph grabbed the headlines when it said: "Will the Philippines remain submissive after China reveals plan to establish 2 new districts in West Philippine Sea?" by Jo-Est B. Tan. **It said quote** On Friday, Filipinos were upset when the Chinese People's Liberation Army stated on their website that Beijing will be setting up two new districts in Paracels and Spratly Islands and will be under the control of Sansha City. The Nansha District will be handling the Spratly Islands, and the areas surrounding it. Its government will hold office on Yongshu Jiao, China's name for Philippine-claimed Fiery Cross (Kagitingan) Reef. On the other hand, it will be the Xisha District's responsibility to supervise Paracel Islands, the Maccles-field Bank, and other nearby areas. Unquote. Upon hearing of this news, Vietnam immediately filed a protest against China but the Philippines remained silent. For details visit Website below

https://www.msn.com/en-ph/news/national/will-the-philippines-remain-submissive -after-china-reveals-plan-to-estab-

lish-2new-districts-in-west-phillipine-sea/ar-BB12WeAi?li=BBrBMkn

This is the photo that accompanied that news

I was already done writing the draft copy of this book when another item appeared today April 28, 2020 from msn.com/en-ph and it shocked me, because it reads: "**Palace disagrees with US on China using COVID-19 pandemic to push territorial ambitions.**" Right now, I am so perplexed on where and what direction the Philippines is being led into by President Duterte because if he is sulking from the US because President Trump does not give him the attention that China is giving him (Duterte). the Philippine should wake up and act now because the real target of China is not its friendship with the Philippines but to grab more territories from us.

Let me show you some pictures of why I am so concerned with China's suspicious moves:

Similar Photo appears on Chapter 18 page 47

The south seas is being patrolled by China's Coast Guard like the above photo. Naval artillery ships are moored inside their fully developed naval base.

China's Naval Base under construction

Photo of China's naval base nearing completion

One of China's completed settlement.

Photo of China's high-technology communication Station. Radars and antennae are covered by a dome (radome)

While China is building 2 cities plus a complete Naval base, drilling for oil is continuously going on.

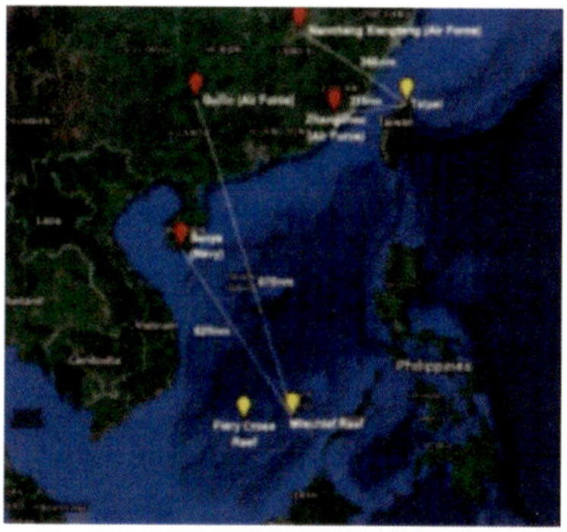

General Map of the area, showing the whole region

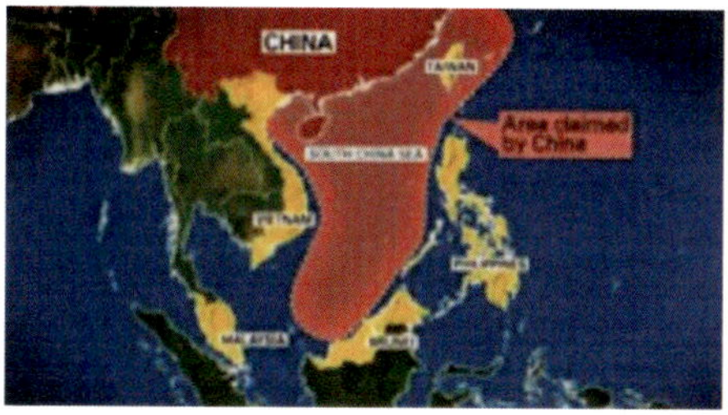

Map showing the master plan of China

My fellowmen, although I have long been an American citizen, I am still addressing you as "my fellowmen" because the Philippines is still my native land. And my main purpose of writing this book is to awaken you and then convince you to consider the Philippines becoming a part of America again. I'm using the word *again* because the Philippines was once part of the US until we asked them for independence because of our deep nationalistic values. We thought it was alright for the Philippines to be run like hell under the Filipino leadership than to be run like heaven under the Americans. Then after we got independent, we drove the US military away and dismantled their

Air and Naval bases because we wanted to appease the communist people who were all anti Americans.

But where are these communist now? Are they depending us from the Chinese who are grabbing our lands or are they the advance party of China? So, if somebody will run as the flag bearer of Statehood USA movement you must support and vote for him or her.

Please bear in mind that China is already at our doorstep and yet we seem to be still asleep. Therefore, I plea to you, wake up Philippines, please wake up.

Chapter 24

Advantages for the United States and the Philippines with this Movement

As I have mentioned to you in my Foreword on page 2, this Statehood movement of the Philippines into the United States would not only be beneficial to the Philippines and to the United States but to the majority of the world as well.

There will be countless of advantages over the disadvantages, so what I will show to you are just the most obvious ones; and they are as follows:

Stability in the Asia-Pacific region. Everybody knows that China wants to dominate the world. Its recent construction of a 'lighthouse at the Spratly on the guise of giving aid to fishermen-in-distress but had turned out just to be the opposite because China is there to scare them by destroying their fishing boats, is a clear manifestation of their evil desire to be the king of the world. But with the Philippines' becoming now a state of the US, the naval base at Olongapo City (*see map on page 69*) which use to be the home port of the US 7th Fleet before they were driven away by the previous administration of the Philippine

Government, will now play as a watchdog to stop China's blatant abuse of their power.

Savings in US money. Since the Philippines will not be purchased from any country, the money saved could be used to improved infrastructure of the US and the Philippines.

The return to the Philippines of the island in Spratly that was grabbed by China (*see map on p47*)

Peaceful Resolution of the overlapping claims by six nations composed of Philippines, Taiwan, China, Malaysia, Vietnam, and Brunei. https://www.theatlantic.com/magazine/archive/1987/ll/a-damaged-culture/505178/

The return to the Philippines of the islands in Spratly that was grabbed by China (*see map on p47 & p61*)

The everlasting threat of China to Taiwan will be stopped because the US will be standing nearby.

Corruption and abuse of power in the Philippines will be minimized if not stopped.

Population explosion will be under check, religious influence will be minimized because separation of state and the church is strongly observed in the US.

Reduction of the US's import of tropical agricultural produce from other countries because the Philippines would now supply the needs of mainland USA.

Terrorist group in the Philippines like the abusayaf will be stopped.

Smuggling will be halted because US Coast Guard will constantly patrol the Philippine seas

US 7th Fleet (or other Naval Fleets) will once again find a home port in the Philippines.

Standard of living will be lifted, and poverty will vanish in the Philippines.

Almost if not all rebels will come back into the society.

Philippine Currency will be converted into US dollars.

USA Healthcare system will now be enjoyed by Filipinos.

Everyone now will have a **Social Security pension** once they reach a senior citizens' age-level.

Presidential position in the Philippines will be downgraded to Governor General.

Department of Foreign Affairs in the Philippines will be phased out.

School System will be systematized. College Graduates will no longer take exams like ECFMG or the Educational Commission for Foreign Medical Graduates, or NCLEX (National Council Licensure Examination) and other board exams because they now belong to the US.

The Philippine Military Academy will now be directly affiliated with **West Point. Philippines will be decongested** of its over-population because some folks could migrate to other states needing people to work in the farms.

There are quite a lot more advantages that could be written herein, but I will leave them to you to visualize because it is indeed true that this move will be beneficial to most parts of the world.

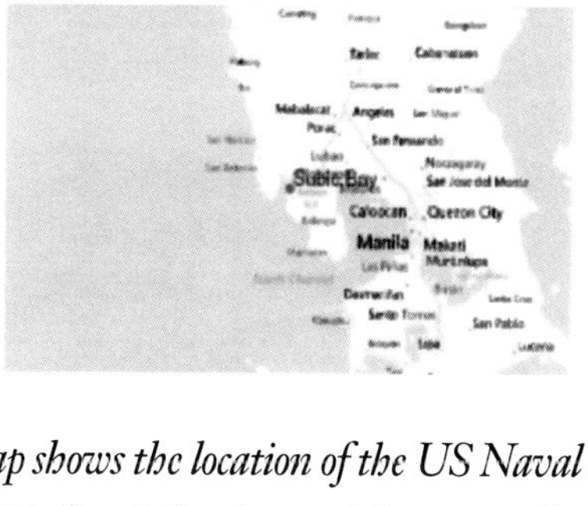

The above map shows the location of the US Naval base in Subic Bay (home port of the 7th fleet before it was driven away by the Philippines in previous administration as the NPA and other rebels were rejoicing)

Chapter 25

What Shall We Do Now? Too Late the Hero?

I am an American citizen, so I cannot vote in any Philippine Election. But granting I was qualified to vote, would have chosen Miriam Defensor Santiago as my President, leaving behind Grace Poe, Mar Rojas, Rodrigo Duterte and Jejomar Binay. But because I am a law-abiding citizen, I will respect one hundred percent, whoever was chosen by the people as their President.

Today we are merely two years away from the next Philippine presidential election which will be on the 9th of May 2022, and I can only hope there will be somebody brave enough to declare and create a party for Statehood USA. Meantime we have to focus on China, on what they are constructing at the Spratly Islands. And at the rate China is going, two years is quite a good period of time for them to build any kind of infrastructure according to their master plan of building two modern cities called Yongshu Jiao (Kagitingan) and Nansha District (see page 60).

So, what should the Philippines do now? Are we already late? Yes, we are already late, because we should have acted to

stop their construction right after we discovered their plans in 2016. But we did nothing to stop them or at least delay their actions. Instead, the Philippines befriended them. I cannot understand why the Philippines is so **beholden** to China. Look at the cowardice actions that the Philippines is doing, whenever there is a naval exercise that the US, Japan make, the Philippines will at once release a "note verbal" condemning the exercise because it will create disapproval from China. I cannot understand what kind of foreign relations we have.

Let me again repeat the question I wrote earlier just to emphasize my grave concern on the situation we are in right now. Are we already late? Yes, we are late, but better late than never. Then what shall we do? First, President Duterte must (1) Stop asking employment from China. Then communicate with President Trump so more Filipinos could work in the US. The US likes documented workers more than the undocumented illegal aliens who sneak through the US-Mexican border. For the information of everyone, according to the world bank, five months in the year 2018 alone, $33.8 billion US dollars was remitted to the Philippines by Filipino workers in the US. (2) If the Philippines is afraid to get the ire of China, then we must cultivate a stronger relationship with Vietnam because they are the country who is not afraid of China. We will let them do the starring role and let the Philippines be the supporting actor in protesting against the hostile attitude of China. (3) Philippines should urge Vietnam and Taiwan to communicate with the US and spearhead a naval exercise at the Spratly areas regularly (4) Let Vietnam bring their protest to the international court of justice. (5) Borrow money from the world bank to explore the Spratly Islands for oil (5) Vietnam Coast guard and the Philippine Navy must navigate the Spratly areas side by side to make

their presence stronger. We should always bear in mind though that in 1975 South Vietnam (before it fell to North Vietnam) maneuvered the Filipinos to leave Pugad Island to attend a birthday party in another island. When They returned, the island was already occupied by South Vietnamese Soldiers.

https://en.wikipedia.org/wiki/Philippians_and_the_Spratty_Islands

CHAPTER 26

Breaking News!

I bringing to you verbatim, the whole news clip of today's headlines from msn.com/en-ph so you will feel the gravity of the situation over at the Spratlys group of islands which the Philippines just seems to ignore.

Quote
Daily Mail

© Provided by Daily Mail China has taken advantage of the world's struggle with Covid-19 to mount a disturbing display of military firepower and push its illegal claims to land and oilfields in a two-million-square-mile area in the South China Sea

China flexes its military muscle: Beijing exploits COVID crisis to assert control of strategically vital South China Sea - and the US sends three warships in response Mark Nicol Defense Editor For The Mall On Sunday today May 9, 2020

China has taken advantage of the world's struggle with Covid-19 to mount a disturbing display of military firepower and push its illegal claims to land and oilfields in a two-million-square-mile area in the South China Sea. The moves have triggered an immediate response from US President Donald Trump. Deeply worried about Beijing's insatiable desire for land and the way its military has occupied areas by stealth, Washington has sent three warships to the region.

China's escalation of war games in the region follows decades of aggression by the Communist government.

© Provided by Daily Mall China has taken advantage of the world's struggle with Covid-19 to mount a disturbing display of military firepower and push its illegal claims to land and oilfields in a two-million-square-mile area in the South China Sea

Breaking News!

It is ignoring international law as it militarizes islands and reefs, plans to exploit oil and mineral fields, and hopes to build nuclear reactors in the area.

No wonder experts fear the South China Sea is where a war involving China, the United States and Russia could begin. China's defense minister, General Wei Fenghe, has said his country would "fight at all costs" if a war occurred with America.

Neighboring nations Malaysia, the Philippines, Vietnam, Taiwan and Brunei have all become embroiled in the crisis. The

South China Sea is vital to the global economy. It contains the world's most lucrative shipping lanes, carrying trade worth about £3.4 trillion a year. An estimated 12 per cent of Britain's seaborne trade—£97 billion of imports and exports a year—passes through the region.

The dispute over the region dates back to 1947 when, in the wake of Japan's surrender in 1945, Beijing drew up a so-called Nine-Dash line, marking out the 90 percent of the South China Sea over which it claims sovereignty.

© Provided by Daily Mail The moves have triggered an immediate response from US President Donald Trump. Deeply worried about Beijing's insatiable desire for land and the way its military has occupied areas by stealth, Washington has sent three warships to the region

Provided by Daily Mail

The moves have triggered an immediate response from US President Donald Trump. Deeply worried about Beijing's insatiable desire for land and the way its military has occupied areas by stealth, Washington has sent three warships to the region.

This infuriated other countries—they complain that the UN Convention on the Law of the Sea is being flouted.

Central to the dispute our nations' rival claims ownership of the Spratly and Paracel archipelagos. Whichever country owns these islands can lay claim to the waters and resources around them.

China has transformed three disputed tidal reefs into military bases. Satellite pictures show substantial infrastructure on the "Big Three" reefs—Subi, Mischief and Fiery Cross.

Another airfield on Woody Island is equipped with missiles, while fighter jets and radar systems have also been stationed there. With a furious President Trump saying the COVID-19 virus has hit the US harder than the Japanese bombing of Pearl Harbor and blaming China for the pandemic, the situation can only get worse....

© Provided by Daily Mail The guided missile cruiser USS Bunker Hill, front, and the Arleigh Burke-class guided-missile destroyer USS Barry (DDG-52) are pictured above in the South China Sea last month

Provided by Daily Mail The guided missile cruiser USS Bunker Hill, front, and the Arleigh Burke-class guided-missile destroyer USS Barry (DDG-52) are pictured above in the South China Sea last month

Unquote

CHAPTER 27

Looking Back

In times like this, where China's belligerent attitude is the common topic in our everyday lives, double take if you are an Asian because of China's extremely ruthless attitude over at the Spratly's group of islands, ramming over fishing-boats with their naval vessels, I cannot help but look back at the 197 house members who opposed President Clinton's heavy lobbying at congress for the inclusion of China as a founding member of WTO. (*see Chap 19: Debt of gratitude pp 50-52*).

Let me refresh your memory into the years 1998 when President Bill Clinton visited China for ten days, (the longest visit by any US President). Upon his return, he lobbied heavily to bring China into WTO as a founding member. Before I go on, let me address to you two issues, namely: why did Clinton stayed ten days in China? There was no direct answer to this question but in my research, it was to get away from the stormy discussions at the lower house on his impeachment, (he was the second President to be impeached). And secondly, why did Clinton lobby so strongly in favor of China's direct inclusion

in WTO. Probable answer was, he wanted to remove the red mark in his career as an impeached President and instead to be remembered as the US President instrumental in putting China into the annals of WTO history.

Did he receive any reward from China? I don't know, but on the news clip written by Reed Irvine and Cliff Kincaid (https://www.aim.org/media-monitor/clintons-china-scandals/) it mentioned a company donating big money to Clinton's party. Then it alluded to Clinton's willingness to transfer sensitive Aerospace data after receiving that donation. It was claimed that classified information helped China reprogram their rocket and missiles engineering design which at that time suffered numerous failures at their launch pads during takeoff into a modern technology it is today. After investigation, Loral company was penalized by $14 million for this transgression.

What would have happened if China was not sponsored by (Clinton) the US into WTO? I can only guess. but the most logical answer is China would not have been rich as quickly as it is now.

Without a doubt, unlike the US where its wealth is used to buy, build and help people in need, China's wealth is being used to buy, build and bully the weaklings. If you are a weak nation and you criticize China, then you better be on the lookout, because somehow, China will retaliate on you. The news spread of April 6, 2020 said that China felt insulted on the comment by one of Brazil's minister about this corona virus pandemic, And China is demanding an explanation from Brazil why they did so, which is short of asking Brazil to apologize to them. See website listed below.

https://www.msn.com/en-ph/news/world/brazil-minister-offends-china-with-racist-virus-tweet/ar-BB12fcyG?li=

BBr8Mkn&ocid=ocid=cbrecir And the only way to neutralize China's belligerent attitude is for the US presence to be felt in this Asia-Pacific region by way of the Philippines becoming a state of the US.

However, bear in mind that this China problem is not the only reason that I am advocating the Philippine Statehood USA movement, because believe you me, there are tons of advantages to be gained by both the US and the Philippines including the almost all countries in the world once the Philippines becomes part of the US.

And before I end this book, I must tell you that someone should religiously initiate this move, so the people of the Philippines could vote for it. And if this movement will win in the Philippines, I am sure without doubt that government of the United States will approve it in a heartbeat.

Chapter 28

Maybe They Were Right

When President Bill Clinton started lobbying for China to be included as a founding member of WTO, the initial count in congress was an overwhelming "no." However, after so many speeches in states where its congressmen were against it, the final count became favorable to Clinton with the house voting 237 in favor and 197 in disagreement (with one abstaining to vote), On the other hand, outside congress, the United Automakers were vehemently against it. (see page 51) More than this, the European countries as well as Japan were also concerned of China's joining WTO without first doing some changes in its tariff policies. But did China make some reforms? From the start "yes," but it was noticed by a businessman in the person of Donald Trump that China was doing currency manipulation to the disadvantage of the US. Let me present to you a news clip from CNBC about WTO archaic rules. It says, quote:

'A reform-or-die moment': Why World Powers want to change the WTO. Published 02272020

The United States, Europe and China have clashed over trade policy for several years and tensions could continue for decades without serious reform, experts have told CNBC.

One of the most contentious points is the future of the World Trade Organization (WTO)—an intergovernmental institution that regulates international trade practices. President Donald Trump has called the WTO "broken," saying countries such as China have taken advantage of it. The US has also threatened to leave.

Speaking last month at the World Economic Forum in Davos, Switzerland. Trump said the WTO has been very unfair to the United States for many, many years. And without it, China wouldn't be China, and China wouldn't be where they are right now." Standing right next to the President. Meanwhile WTO Director General Ricardo Azevedo accepted that it "has to be updated. It has to be changed. It has to be reformed." Unquote.

While commerce seems to be the center stage in this discussion, we must not forget that the other arm of China is secretly focused on their ruthless militarization. Protests over China's belligerent behavior at the China Seas, had been mounting. Scholars are quite concerned now more than ever regarding the bullying tactics of China.

Classified reports made by Pentagon confirms these hostile activities of China. This brings me now to an educated analysis, that maybe the 197 congressmen, the United Automakers, the European countries, Japan, and all the scholars who evaluated China led by Michael Pillsbury, maybe they were right.

Afterword

The precursor signs are bad. With these foreboding events happening left and right, I can tell you that we are heading straight into a perfect storm.

What shall we do then? Let me repeat to you what I wrote in the previous page (p78) that in my studies, in my research, and in my experience, the only remedy to this escalating and worsening situation is for the US's presence to be felt again in Asia. And how could this be accomplished? This could be done in two ways, namely:

(1) The palliative way: Invite the US to rent a space to permanently put up both a Naval and Airbase again in the Philippines. As usual, this move will invite criticism from the communist party and the NPA; from the elites who believes in themselves; and from the Catholic religious groups. But we have to ignore them for the sake of obtaining peace.

(2) The permanent way: let the Philippines be a State of the US.

Remember that whichever action is taken, there will always be some groups who will be against this move; they will be strong and rebellious because they have money to spend financed by China.

I therefore urge everyone to be objective and choose the permanent solution because this is the best for all mankind.

Finally, do not be afraid of war because there will be no war; all we need is to be strong, because there is peace in strength. Remember what is said in page 27 chapter 11, we need to be strong but humble, so you will get the respect of other nations.

Acknowledgment

Note: I've decided to write down the two-liner websites right after the topic in its respective chapters. However, the longer ones are written below. Details of maps can be viewed came from websites herein:

https://imagessearch.yahoo.com/yhs/search?p=philiopine+ map&fr = yhs-symantec-ext onb&hspart=symantec&hsimp=yhs-ext onb&imgurl=https%302F%2Fimages.search,yahoo.com%2F search%2F, mages963Fp%3Dohiliopine%2Bmap& gig con-sent skip=1586565996#id=11 tmurl=htto%3A%2F%2F3,bp.blogspotcom%2F d13803x0LHSU%2FSaaLkVAF2- 1%2FAAAAAAAA-AINIA9(2FpX2aVXju7NM%2Fs16011%2Fohilippine map.gif&act ion=click

https://images.search.yahoo.com/yhs/search?p=map+of+subic + bay+ p tiilipoines 84fr=yhs-syrnantec-ext onb&hspart=sy mentec8thsimp—Iyhs-ext onb&irngurl=http%3A9'02F%2Fwafast-meteo.com962Flo-

cationmaps%2FSubic-
Bay.13.9if& guc
consent skip=,1586567643#id=108tiuri=htto%3A%2F%
2FwG.fast-meteo.com%2Flocationmaps962FSubic-
Bay.8.gif&action=click

httpsAmages.search.yahoo.com/yhs/search?p=map+sbratly÷isl
ands&fr=y hs-symantec-ext
onb&hspart=.symantec8thsirnp=yhs¬ext
onb&imgurl=https%3A%2F%2Fupload.wikimedia.org%2Fw
ikipedia%2Fc ommons%2F8%2F8f%2FSpratly isiands-
DA Wf8 Map.png& guc consent
skip=1586567792#id=18tiurl=http%3A% 2F%2F4.bp.blog-
spot.c om%2F-Eflyesp1s0A962FTr-
ilLSZHKr1%2FAAAAAAAAAJw962F60c003tLyMU962Fs16
00%2Fspratly-islands-l.gif&action=click

For details about Oil refer to websites below:
https://search.yahoo.com/yhs/search?hspart=pty&hsimp=yhs-
pty email&param2=ae7037d8-a884-4fee-9e97-
634d364120848<param3=email —US—appfocus1-
&param4=d-ccc4- lp0-dsf email-cp 6645210473-tst0—
bb8—Chrome—date+crude+oil+was+discovered-
0AFF2980240C75759
FF8 142AA7F91576&param1=20200412&p=date+crude+oil-
was+disc overed&type=em abbfocusl cr-asec-

and

https://search.yahoo.com/yhstsearch?hspart=ptv&hsimo=yhs
¬pty email&param2=ae7037d8-a8B4-4fee-9e97-

634d3641 2084 &param 3=email —US—appfocus1-8,&param4=d-ccc4- lp0-dsfemail-cp 6645210473-tst0—bb88—Chrome—who+discovered+commercial+oil+in+middle+east—0AF

and
https://search.yahoo.com/yhs/search?hspart=pty&hsimp=yhs-pty email&param2=ae7037d8-a884-4fee-9e97-634d36412084&param3=email -US-appfocus1-&param4=d ccc4 -lp0-dsf email-c& 6645210473-tst0- bb8-Chrome—who+discovered+commercial+oil+in+middle+east-OAF F2960240C75759FF8142AA7F915768param1=20200412&p =who+di scoyered+commercial+oil+in+middle-east&type=em appfocusl cr-asec-

Details about Spratlys islands:
https://en.wikipedia.org/wiki/Free Territory of Freedomlad
https://en.wikipedia.org/wiki/Spratly Islands dispute
https://www manilatimes net/2018/08/13/opinion/columnists/ topanalysis/revealed-marcos-secret-operations-to-take-over-entire-spratly-archipelago/429769/429769/
https://opinion.inquirer net/6789/the-spratlys-marcos%E2%80%99-legacy-or-curse
https://www youtube com/watch?v=NOUKTKiMPEO

https://enwikipedia.org/wiki/Free Territory of Freedomland
https://en.wikipedia.org/wiki/Spratly Islands dispute
https://www.manilatimes.net/2018/013/13/opinion/columnists/topanalysis/revealed-marcos-secret-operations-to-take-over-entire spratly archipelago/429769/429769/
https.//opinion.inquirer net/6789/the-spratlys-

marcos%E2%80%99- legacy-or-curse
https.//www youtube.com/watch?v=NOUKTKiMPEO

About Tomas Cloma:
https://en.wikipedia.org/w}ki/Free Territory of Freedomland
https://en wikipedia.org/wiki/Spratly Islands dispute
https://www.manilatinnes net/2018/08/13/opinion/columnist
s/topanalysis/revealed-marcos-secret-operations-to-take-
over-entire-spratly-archipelago/429769/429769/ httpsi/opin-
ion.inouirer
net/6789/the-spratlys-nnarcos%Er/080°/099-legacy7or-curse
https://www.youtube.com/watch?v—-NOUKTNMPEO

China's scandals:
https://search.yahoo. com/yhs/search?hspart=pty&hsim
p=yhs-pty email&param2=ae7037d8-a884-4fee-9e97-
634d36412084&param3=email -US-appfocus1-&param4=d-
ccc4-10-dsf email-cp 6645210473-tst0— bb8-Chrome-
what+is+hullabalo-OAFF2960240C75759FF8142A
A7F91576&param1=2020041280=what+is+hullabalo&type=e
m appfocus1 cr-athi-
https://www.washingtonexaminer.com/clinton-foundation-
scandal-echoes-clinton-china-controyersy-from-1998

https://www.nationalreview.com/2017/07/chinese-illegally-
donated-bill-clinton-reelection-campaign-media-down-
plaved/
https://www.aim.ord/media-monitor/clintons-china-scandals/

Billionaires in China;
https://www.bloomberg.com/news/articles/2018-11-29/why-

communist-china-is-home-to-so-many-billionaires-quicktake

Make China great again:
https://www.msn.com/en-ph/news/world/how-china-is-ruthlessly-exploiting-the-coronavirus-pandemic-it-helped-cause/ar-BB13kKQH?li=BBr8Mkn&ocid=-cbrecir

Philippines submissive to China:
https://www.msn.com/en-ph/news/national/will-the-philippians-remain-submissiveafter-china-reveals-plan-to-establish-2-new-districts-in-west-philippine-sea/ar-BB12WeAi?li=BBr8Mkn

Breaking News!
https ://www. msn com/en-ph/news/world/china-flexes-its-military-muscle-beijing-exploits-covid-crisis-to-assert-control-of-strategically-vital-south-china-sea-and-the-us-sends-three-warships-in-response/ar-BB13QWV9?li=BBr8zL6

WTO:
https://en.wikipedia.org/wiki/China_and the World Trade Organization_ https://www.cnbc.com/2020/02/07/world-powers-us-eu-china-are-grappling-to-update-the-wto.html

China vs the US
https://www.msn.com/en-ph/news/world/us-would-lose-a-war-with-china-fought-in-the-pacific-is-unable-to-defend-taiwan-from-an-invasion-and-there-are-fears-the-guam-military-base-is-at-risk-now-pentagon-sources-warn/ar-BB14bKMa?li=BBr8Mkn

Damaged culture:
http://whynationsfail.com/blog/2012/12/13/a-damaged-culture. html

If you are in favor of this "Philippine Statehood USA" movement, send me with your comments, suggestions and or recommendations. My contact email address is:

oscarsalazarabejo@hotmail.com

** God Bless the Philippines and God Bless the United States of America**